Scarecrow Christmas!

by Alison Hedger
A new children's musical with six delightful songs.

Approximate duration 30 minutes.

Suitable for Early years and Key Stage 1.
Also useful for slightly older children in after-school clubs,
where fun can be had putting on an "al fresco" presentation.

Teacher's Book complete with CD.

Production notes, story, song lyrics
and music with chord symbols included.

SONGS

1. Scrub-A-Dub-Dub
2. Silver Fish (song and dance)
3. Hairy Bears (song and dance)
4. Yellow Feathered Ducklings (song and dance)
5. Teeny-Weeny Red Suit
6. It's Christmas!

This musical has no particular religious affinities, and is for all children to enjoy.
The storyline depicts an ideal where concern for others is the accepted social behaviour.

Illustrations by Hilary Black.

A licence should be obtained from Music Sales Limited for performances of this work.

© Copyright 2002 Golden Apple Productions
A division of Chester Music Limited
14-15 Berners Street, London W1T 3LJ, UK.

Order No. GA11363

ISBN 978-0-7119-9158-3

Although Scarecrow needs and receives warm coats from kind-hearted friends, he unselfishly gives them away to others whom he feels need them more than himself, so benefiting everyone.

Woven around this story, is the funny situation that Mrs Christmas and her helping elves have shrunken Santa's party outfit! Will he be cross . . . ? No, he too shows generosity, and gives his shrunken suit to Scarecrow, to keep him warm. All ends in a riotous Christmas party!

CAST LIST

*indicates some speaking

Narrator(s)
*Scarecrow
*Mrs Christmas
Helping Elves
Silver Fish   (dance)
*Moon
Polar Bears   (dance)
*Cloud
Ducklings   (dance)
*Sun
*Santa

COSTUMES

(Much can be achieved with card, paper and paint. It is not necessary to fully costume the cast, as often an appropriate hat/head-dress will suffice. The list below is ideal, but not ultimately necessary.)

To achieve the maximum visual effect, use the brightest colours possible (except for the Moon, Cloud and Sun who are dull, until they put on their special coats).

- Scarecrow is brightly, yet scantily dressed.
- Mrs Christmas and Santa are dressed all in red.
- A suit of red "Santa" clothes will be needed for Scarecrow.
- The helping elves are in green.
- The fish are silver/grey.
- The polar bears are dressed all in white (nylon fur at wrists and ankles, if whole fur costumes are out of the question!)
- The ducklings are in yellow (some feathers if at all possible!)

PROPS

- Wash tub (a coloured baby bath).
- A large over-sized red "Santa" suit to be "washed".
- Washing line strung between two poles, with a small set of "Santa" clothes pegged up with brightly coloured pegs.
- Three coats for Scarecrow to wear and give away: silver, white, yellow.

  The coats could be sleeve-less body warmers. If at all possible, the different textures of scales, fur and feathers should be a feature.
- Sleigh Bells.

SET

No set is necessary, but if appropriate, a wintry, snowy scene is all that is needed.

MUSIC and DANCES

The accompanying CD has all you need for rehearsals and performances, with the songs sung, and also presented as backing tracks.

The dances need only be very simple indeed. It is more important to convey the fish/bear/duckling characteristics of movement, rather than choreograph a splendid dance routine!

Wintry sound effects are included on the CD. Each time Scarecrow feels the cold, there could be some icy metallic sounds from percussion instruments. However, don't use Sleigh Bells, as these are best saved for heralding Santa.

This page is blank for your own production notes

This page is blank for your own production notes

SCARECROW'S CHRISTMAS!

Opens with Scarecrow on stage, shivering in an imaginary cold wind. He is standing in snow and ice. (Wintry sound effects are on the matching CD.)

Narration: Scarecrow lived all alone. He wasn't bothered about being alone, but what he didn't like was being cold. How he longed for warm sunshine on his back, and a gentle spring breeze on his face. But all he got today was icy blasts of winter winds and grey skies overhead! He wished very hard that he could be warm. What a way to spend Christmas Day – frozen cold!

Scarecrow moves to one side and Mrs Christmas enters carrying a large red Santa suit. She is followed by her helping elves, carrying a washing tub.

Narration: Mrs Christmas and her helping elves are going to wash Santa's red outfit, ready for their Christmas Day party later that afternoon.

SONG ONE   SCRUB-A-DUB-DUB

Make appropriate actions throughout

Verse 1:

Scrub-a-dub-dub,
We'll slosh in this tub,
The suds will splish and splat!
We're working hard
In our backyard,
We're washing Santa's hat.
Lots of water to rinse away the soap.
Now it's time to wash his coat.

Verse 2:

Wring the coat
And dripping hat,
We'll twist them hard and lay them flat.
The trousers we will dunk and wash.
You know how we just love to splosh!

Verse 3:

Scrub-a-dub-dub,
We've sloshed in this tub,
The washing's all been done.
We've finished cleaning Santa's clothes.
My word! It has been fun! HEY!

Mrs Christmas: Come on helpers. Let's go and hang these wet clothes up to dry.

Mrs Christmas and her helping elves exit, taking their washing and wash tub with them.

Narration: Scarecrow stood alone and shivered, knocking his knees together. He wished hard that he was warm. Just then some beautiful silver fish swam alongside him. They thought Scarecrow looked very cold and sad for Christmas Day.

Scarecrow: You look sleek and happy in your beautiful silver coats.

Narration:	The fish nodded. Yes, they didn't feel the cold. Then they had a brilliant idea. They would give Scarecrow one of their coats to stop his knees knocking together, then they would cheer him up with a fantastic swooping fishy dance.

SONG TWO   **SILVER FISH**

With a swish we're dancing round in circles,
We're fish as you can see.
Silver scales that twinkle in the water,
Are tiny and shiny,
And special as metal,
Just right to warm Scarecrow's cold knees!

The music is repeated for a swishing fishy dance, during which a long silver coat is given to Scarecrow, who puts it on. The fish exit leaving Scarecrow all alone, feeling much warmer.

Narration:	As Scarecrow was enjoying his new coat, a dark and dull moon came up to him.

Scarecrow:	Oh Moon, you don't look at all shiny. Here, take my new coat, it should help you glow, so that everyone can enjoy your silver light on Christmas night.

The Moon takes the coat and puts it on. This makes him feel bright and happy.

Moon:	Thank you Scarecrow!

Moon exits leaving Scarecrow all alone. He once again feels the cold, and he shivers from top to toe.

Narration: Scarecrow stood all alone. He felt cold again. He wished he could be warm. Just then some white polar bears lumbered up to him. They thought Scarecrow shouldn't be so cold on Christmas Day.

Scarecrow: You look nice and warm in your fur coats.

Narration: The bears nodded. Yes, they didn't feel the cold. Then they had a brilliant idea. They would give him one of their coats to make him as warm as they were. They wanted to entertain Scarecrow with a bumbling bear dance.

SONG THREE   # HAIRY BEARS

We are very hairy bears,
Covered in fur that is silky white.
We keep warm in snow and ice,
We don't get cold at midnight.

Ev'ry bear that has been born,
Lived his life so very warm.
We will give to Scarecrow there,
One of our coats that we have to spare!

The music is repeated for a lumbering bear dance, during which a white fur coat is given to Scarecrow, who puts it on. The bears exit leaving Scarecrow all alone, feeling much warmer.

Narration: As Scarecrow was enjoying his new fur coat, a grey and drab cloud came alongside him.

Scarecrow: Oh Cloud, you're not at all white and fluffy. Here, take my new coat, it should help take away that grey feeling. We don't want rain on Christmas Day.

The cloud takes the white coat and puts it on. This makes him very happy.

Cloud: Thank you Scarecrow!

Cloud exits leaving Scarecrow all alone. He once again starts to feel cold and he begins to shiver.

Narration: Scarecrow stood alone and began to shiver. He wished hard that he was warm. Just then some yellow ducklings waddled past. They thought Scarecrow looked too cold to enjoy Christmas Day.

Scarecrow: You look warm in your yellow fluffy coats.

Narration: The ducklings nodded. Yes, they were beautifully warm, but they were sorry that Scarecrow was cold. Then they had a brilliant idea. They would give him one of their coats to keep him warm, and then they would make him laugh, with one of their funny dances!

SONG FOUR YELLOW FEATHERED DUCKLINGS

Poor old Scarecrow,
He is cold and he is glum.
Poor old Scarecrow,
He is sad without the sun.
We will give him a fluffy coat.
Front and back and arms and throat
Will warm quickly.
He'll keep really cosy,
Whatever the weather,
In lovely yellow feathers! Quack!

The music is repeated for a dance and quacking routine, during which a fluffy yellow coat is given to Scarecrow, who puts it on. After the dance, the ducklings waddle off, leaving Scarecrow alone, feeling much warmer.

Narration: As Scarecrow was enjoying his yellow coat, a dismal and dull sun came up to him.

Scarecrow: Oh Sun, you don't look very happy. You are supposed to shine golden yellow and make everything nice and warm, especially this afternoon at Santa's Christmas party. Here, take my new coat.

Scarecrow takes off his coat and Sun puts it on. This makes him bright and happy.

Sun: Thank you Scarecrow!

Sun exits leaving Scarecrow alone.

Narration: Scarecrow had given three warm coats away. Now he wondered if he had perhaps been a little foolish not keeping a warm coat for himself. "No" he thought, "I'm glad the moon will be bright. I'm glad the clouds will be white and I'm glad that the sun will be golden yellow!"
Just then, Mrs Christmas and the helping elves came up to Scarecrow in a frightful tizz-wozz!

Mrs Christmas: Scarecrow, guess what! Something awful has happened.

All the elves echo her words and shake their heads . . .

Something awful has happened!

Mrs Christmas: We have shrunk Santa's best Christmas suit by washing it.
Now he won't be able to wear it at the Christmas party this
afternoon. Take a look!

*A washing line strung between two poles is carried in by two elves. Small red Santa
clothes are pegged to the line. Gasps of horror and shaking of heads from the elves!
Sleigh bells are heard in the distance.*

SONG FIVE

TEENY-WEENY RED SUIT

Verse 1:

It's too small,
It's much too teeny.
Deary me,
It's teeny-weeny.
Look at it,
It's such a sight,
It has got to be too tight.

Santa is a man that's fat,
He can't wear a hat like that!
It will never, ever fit.
Put it on and it will split!
It's too small,
It's much too teeny.
Deary me,
It's teeny-weeny.

Verse 2:

It's too small,
It's much too teeny.
Deary me,
It's teeny-weeny.
Look at it,
It's such a sight,
It has got to be too tight.

Santa is a man that's tall,
He can't wear a suit that small!
It will never, ever fit.
Put it on and it will split!
It's too small,
It's much too teeny.
Deary me,
It's teeny-weeny.

Santa Claus enters during the last part of the song.

Narration: Santa looked as though he might be very cross. He looked at his shrunken clothes.
(*He does*)
Everyone watched him, and waited to see what he would say . . . but we needn't have worried. Santa simply said what he always says . . .

Santa: Ho, ho, ho! Ho, ho, ho!

Narration: Santa wasn't a bit cross. In fact, he thought his suit looked funny! Then he looked at Scarecrow, then back at his shrunken suit . . .

Santa: Scarecrow, you look as though you could do with some extra clothing. Would you like this red suit?
(*points to suit on the line*)

Scarecrow: Yes please!

Narration: So the elves took Scarecrow away . . .
(*they leave the acting area and Scarecrow quickly puts on a suitably sized red Santa suit*)
. . . and Santa and Mrs Christmas called out together . . .

Mr & Mrs Christmas: It's time to start the party.
Let the fun begin!
Everyone is invited.

Narration: Santa was actually glad he didn't have to change into another suit, as he was so comfortable in the one he was wearing!
He was also very glad that Scarecrow would now keep warm, whatever the weather!

As the music begins, the fish, bears and ducklings and Moon, Cloud and Sun in their new coats, elves and Scarecrow (dressed in a red suit) come onto the stage. During the song, there is dancing, hand clapping and general party merriment, with Scarecrow dancing centre stage with Santa Claus and Mrs Christmas. The song should be infectious, and have the audience joining in. Anything goes. After all, this is Santa's Christmas party!

SONG SIX   # IT'S CHRISTMAS!

It's Christmas, it's Christmas,
Let's dance round in a ring.
It's Christmas, it's Christmas,
Let everybody sing.
It's Christmas, it's Christmas,
We've never felt so good.
So clap your hands   *repeat several times*
And tap your toes,
The wind may blow
And we'll have snow,
We'll jump and shout
And dance about,
Because it's Christmas Day!

Everyone waves and shouts . . .

HAPPY CHRISTMAS!

THE END

SONG ONE

SCRUB-A-DUB-DUB

Cue: . . . Christmas Day party later that afternoon.

With energy ♩. = 120

1. Scrub - a - dub - dub,____ we'll____ slosh____ in this tub,____ the

suds will____ splish____ and____ splat!____ We're

working — hard — in — our — back - yard, — we're

washing — Santa's — hat. —

Lots of water to rinse a - way the soap.

Now it's time to wash his — coat. —

Am E
2. Wring the coat and drip - ping hat, we'll
Am E
twist them hard and lay them flat. The
F C
trou - sers we will dunk and wash. You
Dm E Am F♯7
know how we just love to splosh!

Bm   F#

3. Scrub - a - dub - dub,   we've sloshed   in this tub,   the

f

Bm   F#

wash - ing's all   been   done.   We've

G   D

fin - ished clean   - ing   San   - ta's   clothes.   My

Em   F#   Bm

word! It   has   been fun!   HEY!

21

SONG TWO   **SILVER FISH**
                  (Song and dance)

Cue: . . . with a fantastic swooping fishy dance.

With movement ♩ = 180 (♩. = 60 feel one to a bar)

With a swish we're danc - ing round in cir - cles, we're

fish as you can see.

Sil - ver scales that twin - kle in the wa - ter, are

ti - ny and shin - y, and spe - cial as me - tal, just

right to warm Scare - crow's cold knees!

Repeat the music for the dance.

SONG THREE **HAIRY BEARS**
(Song and dance)

Cue: . . . to entertain Scarecrow with a bumbling bear dance.

We are ve - ry hair - y bears, cov-ered in fur that is silk - y white.

We keep warm in snow and ice, we don't get cold at mid - night.

Ev - 'ry bear that has been born, lived his life so ve - ry warm.

We will give to Scare - crow there, one of our coats that we have to spare!

CODA

The song melody is in two halves which can be sung or played, at the same time. If you are using older children they could attempt singing in two parts, or perhaps you could have a descant recorder or ocarina repeatedly playing the second half of the melody.

SONG FOUR   **YELLOW FEATHERED DUCKLINGS**
(Song and dance)

Cue: . . . with one of their funny dances!

Full of humour ♩ = 80

Poor old Scare - crow,___ he is cold and he is glum.

Poor old Scare - crow,___ he is sad with - out the sun.

We will give him a fluf - fy coat.___ Front and back and arms and throat___ will warm quick - ly.___ He'll keep real - ly co - sy, what -

- ev - er the wea - ther, in love - ly yel - low feath - ers! Quack!

Repeat the music for the dance. This should be very funny with the ducks quacking noisily. They bends their knees, flap their "wings" and stick out their behinds.

TEENY-WEENY RED SUIT

Cue: (Sleigh bells are heard in the distance)

Neatly ♩ = 92

Cmaj7

mf

C   Am   C   Am

1. 2. It's too small, it's much too teen - y. Dear - y me, it's teen - y - ween - y.

G   C

Look at it, it's such a sight,___ it has got to be too tight.___

F6   C/E   G7/D   C

San - ta is a man that's fat, he can't wear a hat like that!
San - ta is a man that's tall, he can't wear a suit that small!

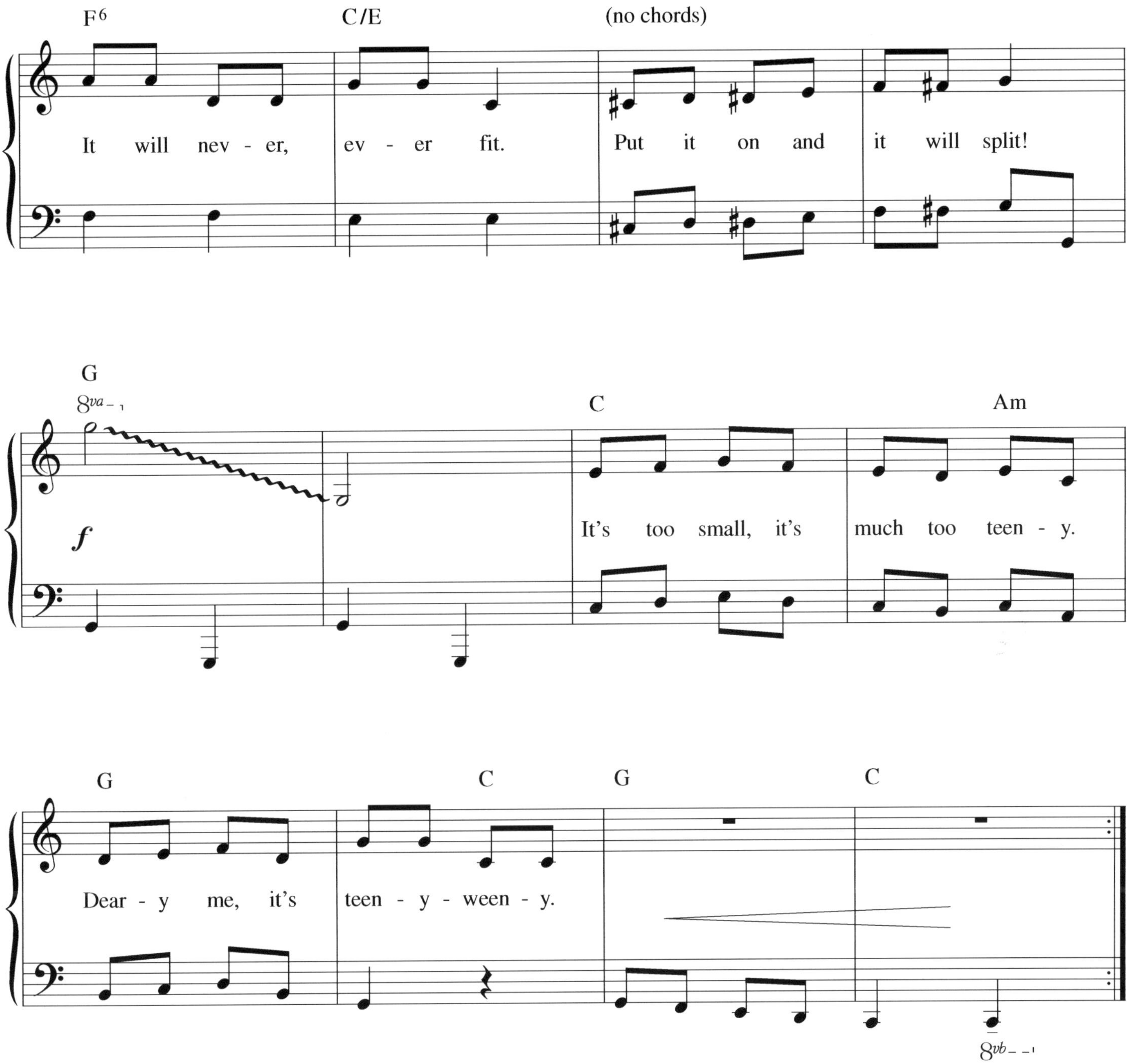
F6 C/E (no chords)
It will nev - er, ev - er fit. Put it on and it will split!
G
8va
f
C Am
It's too small, it's much too teen - y.
G C G C
Dear - y me, it's teen - y - ween - y.
8vb

IT'S CHRISTMAS!

Cue: . . . Scarecrow would now keep warm, whatever the weather!

Very jolly & vivacious ♩ = 120

Christ - mas, it's Christ - mas, let's dance round in a ring. It's

Christ - mas, it's Christ - mas, let ev - 'ry - bo - dy sing. It's

This song should be infectious and have the audience participating with clapping etc.
Anything goes! This is after all, Santa's Christmas party.

10/09 (171686)

CD Track Listing

Complete Songs (with vocals)

1. **Scrub-A-Dub-Dub**
2. **Silver Fish** (song and dance)
3. **Hairy Bears** (song and dance)
4. **Yellow Feathered Ducklings** (song and dance)
5. **Teeny-Weeny Red Suit**
6. **It's Christmas!**

Backing Tracks (vocals omitted)

7. **Scrub-A-Dub-Dub**
8. **Silver Fish** (song and dance)
9. **Hairy Bears** (song and dance)
10. **Yellow Feathered Ducklings** (song and dance)
11. **Teeny-Weeny Red Suit**
12. **It's Christmas!**
13. **SOUND EFFECT- Icy Winds**

Music Arranger
Rick Cardinali

Vocals
Elly Barnes

CD Recorded at Music Sales Limited
London W1